Endorsements

Cheryl Moore has created a unique devotional experience that will awaken an aspect of your being, perhaps most Godlike, your imagination! Unlike vain imaginations, God-inspired imaginations will take you to places of peace and refreshing adventure, enriching your life with every encounter. A significant doorway into a deeper, sweeter, more intimate relationship with God, the ultimate "Imaginator," Cheryl's word pictures inspire and encourage the reader's senses to blossom! Her perseverance and tenacity to complete this work of art the Lord motivated her to begin years ago has now been fulfilled and will bless the lives of many.

LINDA LANGLEY
TRANSFORMATIONS UNLIMITED
GRASS VALLEY, CA

Using our imagination and allowing ourselves to dream with God is often a lost art in our busy and modern world. In her delightful devotional, *Just Imagine*, Cheryl Moore takes us on exciting adventures and stretches our imagination muscles. With every page, and each day's journey, you will be swept into colorful experiences and meaningful encounters with God. Cheryl leads us to explore places with our imaginations, and the result is refreshing for our souls. I highly recommend *Just Imagine* and I know you will be blessed as you read, allowing yourself to encounter God in every beautiful experience.

SYLVIA NEUSCH
SENIOR LEADER, TRUE LIFE FELLOWSHIP
ROUND ROCK, TX
AUTHOR OF *RAGS TO ROYALTY*

Just Imagine

Just Imagine

LIVING IN A
GOD-PAINTED WORLD

An interactive 31-day devotional

*Use your imagination in this interactive
thirty-one-day encounter devotional
designed to give you a taste of living in a
God-painted world where He doesn't
always color inside the lines!*

Cheryl Moore

ELM HILL

**A Division of
HarperCollins Christian Publishing**

www.elmhillbooks.com

Just Imagine
Living in a God-Painted World

Photos used by permission through license purchased from iStockphoto.com and us.fotolia.com

Published in Nashville, Tennessee, by Elm Hill, an imprint of Thomas Nelson. Elm Hill and Thomas Nelson are registered trademarks of HarperCollins Christian Publishing, Inc.

Elm Hill titles may be purchased in bulk for educational, business, fund-raising, or sales promotional use. For information, please e-mail SpecialMarkets@ ThomasNelson.com.

Scripture quotations marked HCSB are from the Holman Christian Standard Bible˚. Copyright © 1999, 2000, 2002, 2003, 2009 by Holman Bible Publishers. Used by permission. HCSB˚ is a federally registered trademark of Holman Bible Publishers.

Scripture quotations marked NIV are from the Holy Bible, New International Version˚, NIV˚. Copyright © 1973, 1978, 1984, 2011 by Biblica, Inc.˚ Used by permission of Zondervan. All rights reserved worldwide. www.Zondervan.com. The "NIV" and "New International Version" are trademarks registered in the United States Patent and Trademark Office by Biblica, Inc.˚

Scripture quotations marked NKJV are from the New King James Version˚. © 1982 by Thomas Nelson. Used by permission. All rights reserved.

Scripture quotations marked NLT are from the Holy Bible, New Living Translation. © 1996, 2004, 2007, 2013, 2015 by Tyndale House Foundation. Used by permission of Tyndale House Publishers, Inc., Carol Stream, Illinois 60188. All rights reserved.

Library of Congress Cataloging-in-Publication Data

Library Control Congress Number: 2018949966

ISBN 978-1-595558053 (Paperback)
ISBN 978-1-595558107 (eBook)

Dedication

To my Abba Father who whispered words into my ear a few years ago saying, "I gave you a very active imagination and I want you to use it to bless others. I gave you the gift of storytelling that has blessed your grandchildren time and time again as you told them bedtime stories." And, although I didn't exactly hear these words, I think He added, "Press in and 'just imagine' what we can write together!"

To my wonderful husband, Don, who has been my champion throughout our married life of over fifty years. His belief in me that I can be more than I thought I could be has pushed me forward to believe in myself and launch this God-sparked book. Thank you for inspiring me and helping me in this project of love. I am eternally grateful to have been given the gift of a husband whose eyes are always on the Lord first and, because of that, he has been the best husband and father in the world. You continue to leave your marks of love on my heart, the hearts of our kids and grandkids, and every person fortunate enough to know you.

To my children, Chad Moore and Amy (Moore) Swearingen, I say thank you too. Both of you used to tell me how great my bedtime stories were and how your own children loved them. You both inspire me and fill me with humility in seeing how you have turned out as grown adults. Both of you and your families are dedicated to Jesus and living lives that leave the footprints of Jesus everywhere you go!

To my seven grandchildren Katie, Megan, Ashley, Luke, Cade, Matt, and Dawson…you are the lights of my life and fill my life with joy, laughter, and love. Each of you has unique gifts from God and I wait in anticipation to see where He leads you as you grow up. LYTTMAB — Love you to the moon and back!

To all of you, my family, thanks for making life a joy and for all the times we spent in laughing until our tummies hurt! Definitely, "Love makes the world go round," but laughter in life makes it all the more glorious!

Acknowledgements

First, I thank God for His prompting that led to this book. I'm so grateful He's such a patient God as it took me several years of "stop" and "go" to finally complete this work of imagination.

To my husband, Don, I bless you for your never-ending encouragement to finish this book. You've always been my champion and you never tired of being my main editor and proofreader. You were so good at offering optional ways to make my message clearer. Thank you, dear husband!

Next, to my graphic-designer daughter, Amy, "thank you" doesn't begin to express how I feel! First, you found Elm Hill Books online…praise God! From the beginning, you've been able to help me "see" the possibilities of how my book could look in actual print. Thank you for the hours you spent with me selecting just the perfect photo to include with each day's reading. Plus, in the final push, you did a sample layout so I could envision what the book might really look like…bringing tears to my eyes! You stayed plugged-in from the beginning to the completion as my technical advisor, being available to help answer design and layout questions that popped up along the way. Thank you, my sweetest Amy, for being such a wonderful, steadfast, loving daughter!

Thank you and huge kudos to the Elm Hill Books team! "Wow!" From my first introduction telephone call to the completion of my book, I was so impressed with the organization of the team. I was pleased to have my own personal "point person" who was assigned to work closely with me during the entire process. Each person I spoke with made me feel like part of their family and sounded like they sincerely wanted to help me produce my book with confidence. They were always available, helpful, and so patient with my many questions! I'll be recommending Elm Hill Books to anyone trying to get their book into print! You've made me feel like a friend, not just a client! Blessings on each of you!

I also want to thank Linda Langley who read my manuscript in order to critique and help edit it from an objective point of view with fresh eyes. Thank you for that special help and for your beautiful endorsement of *Just*

Imagine. Thanks for your love and support for the last thirty years. What a blessing you are!

Finally, thank you, Sylvia Neusch, for taking the time to read my manuscript and write such a special and wonderful endorsement for my book. Your beautiful words fit right in to the theme of *Just Imagine*! I am most grateful to sit under you and your husband, Richard, as my great pastors!

Thank you to everyone, friends and family alike, for your love and encouragement!

Table of Contents

Preface

READ THE DIRECTIONS...

Imagination — is the key to this unique kind of daily devotional book. Let's call it the daily "encounter" book and you can do it in about fifteen minutes or less. After each day's reading, I want you to take a short five-minute "Flight of Fancy" with Papa God and Jesus. Papa God is the supreme *Imaginator*…(I think I just coined a new word!) In our everyday lives, we're forced to live in the reality of the moments of our day. But Jesus wants you to experience your world, Him, the Father, and the Spirit in new ways — using your imagination and your senses. Remember, your imagination is holy, ordained by God since He built it into you. Let's practice using this fabulous gift!

Have you ever looked at this beautiful world we live in and been truly amazed at the creative genius of God — the fingers of God making, molding, designing, and coloring this planet to bless us and our senses, and to give us a place to live and care for? In this thirty-one-day devotional book, I hope you'll be able to get a new sense of the intimate ways God wants to meet you and share with you through your five senses — seeing, hearing, touching, smelling, and tasting.

On most days, I'll ask you to close your eyes and imagine or remember something. You will usually automatically bring something to mind from your past, or you will go to a place of imagination. Then you'll have all the "tools" you need to take a five-minute Flight of Fancy and experience God in new ways. If you have time to do your encounter early in the morning, it may lift your spirit and help give you courage, anticipation, and a new excitement about the day you are about to jump into. Or do this encounter just before bedtime; it can help you reflect on your day in new ways and perhaps spark wonderful dreams, so you awaken tomorrow ready to take on the new day in new ways!

This book is not designed to be read for a specific month, like Day 1 for the first day of a month. Start the book whenever you want and that will be your Day 1. Since it's not date specific, you can feel free to read this book again and again…from beginning to the end, or pick out your favorite day's reading to experience again. Read it however your imagination leads you, **but I suggest that, for the first time through it,** you begin at Day 1 to help set the stage for the following days.

My desire and prayer for you is that, during your quiet encounter time, you rediscover the God-sounds around you and enjoy learning to live in a God-painted, God-fragrant world…a world where He doesn't always color inside the lines!

Perfect Partner

Have you ever tasted an absolutely perfectly ripe mango? If you have, you know the sweetness of the juicy, light yellow-orange fruit. I remember the first time I tasted a really ripe one. It made all the difference in the world when I found the perfect one. Remember your first love, how your heart beat faster and you wanted that special someone to notice you. You believed they were the perfect one for you.

Now I want you to picture yourself as the perfect person whom Jesus is looking for, even though I know you don't think of yourself as perfect. (Men, remember you are the bride of Christ.) You're going to find yourself chosen by Jesus today as His perfect partner. Picture yourself in a big ballroom with lots of other beautiful women forming a circle around the room as they all wait for the Master Dancer to arrive and choose His partner. You're feeling underdressed, a little too pudgy, and you think you're not as beautiful as the rest…so you make your way to the outside of the circle, sort of hidden out of sight.

I've been looking for you, for you are perfect in My sight

Then there He is, the Master Dancer, looking for that perfect partner for the special tango dance. The talking stops as each one waits in anticipation to see if they will be chosen. He walks around the circle several times looking…looking. Then He stops in front of the group where you are "hiding." He bends His head this way and that (do you see this in your mind?). Then He locks eyes with you, reaches between the women in front of you, and takes your hand. He draws you out onto the floor with a look of pure love and joy on His face. You've forgotten about the others as you stare into His eyes. He says, "My daughter, how beautiful you are to Me. I've been looking for you, for you are perfect in my sight. Will you dance with Me?" Here it is, your chance to taste the perfect mango…will you say yes? Suddenly, you realize that the Maker of the universe, your Papa God, your Jesus, has chosen you! You are His special child as you choose Him in return. You dance away in the arms of God, realizing all your worries, anxieties, and need to prove yourself to people are falling away as you sway. Picture your faces, both of you laughing and delighting in this experience of relationship on another level…completely accepted. When the music stops, He places a beautiful crown on your head and says, "Remember, My princess, you are My chosen daughter. I'm always here to take your hand and dance."

You may have heard other people talk about their relationship with Jesus in ways you haven't quite experienced. But today, you've let your imagination take you to a new place with the Lord. Just like when you saw a new variety of mango, you decided to be bold and pay a little more to try one. Your taste buds are forever altered. It's like this now with Jesus. You've entered into a new level and your taste for life will never be the same. You've done the "Mango Tango" with Jesus…don't go back to walking.

Reflection…

_____

_____

_____

_____

_____

Flight of Fancy

I know you've been seeing this in your mind to some degree as you read. But now, close your eyes for five minutes and really put yourself in this picture, see yourself dancing with Jesus and become a daughter of the Master Dancer…Creator of the universe. Remember, you are a royal daughter of the King! Men, remember, you are a son of the King and He wants to partner with you in the same way!

SCRIPTURE

"The royal daughter is all glorious within the palace; her clothing is woven with gold."

PSALM 45:13 (NKJV)

PRAYER

Father, thank you for choosing me to partner with you in our dance of a lifetime.

Explore the New You

*A*s we begin, pause a moment and *imagine* that you are standing in a beautiful forest, surrounded by tall, majestic trees. Are you there yet? Great! Now, we're going to take a deep breath and smell the fragrance of moist earth and tree leaves. It's early morning and the mist is still whispering in the tops of the trees and you can feel the moisture on your face. It's just you, the Lord, a few early birds sounding a morning hello, and the sounds of tiny skittering forest creatures. Today, you are going to explore new options and thoughts that can bring you to a new place in your spiritual life, in a special relationship, or even a new avenue for you to travel.

With all change, there must be the first step. Remember from yesterday that you are a daughter or son of the King and nothing is impossible. It's the **new you!**

Don't be afraid to listen to the whispers of God.

You look around the forest as you try to decide the direction you want to go. There are several different trails you notice as you observe the carpet of leaves beneath your feet. You decide to go straight ahead and see where that leads. You feel the crunch of layers of leaves under your feet and realize that, even if you happen to fall, the landing will be soft! It's like that with your Papa God too — He makes a soft landing for you if you fall.

Now, begin to think about those thoughts you've been putting off as you walk. Look for signs along your path. If the path ahead narrows, are there openings you might miss if you're not watching and walking carefully? As you're walking, talk *out loud* to the Lord. He likes to hear your voice and you also affect the heavenlies by your spoken words. Do you realize that Jesus and you are now talking in a new way? You talk, then you listen to hear His voice in this quiet place. It's okay when you decide to stop. You can pick up this path anytime you want to, or go back to the starting point and try a different direction. Just keep Jesus with you on the trail and keep talking and listening...for He longs to speak to you through new thoughts, images, encounters with others, circumstances, and through His Word. Don't be afraid to listen for the whispers of God in your ears.

Reflection...

_____

_____

_____

_____

_____

Flight of Fancy

Now that you've finished the reading, close your eyes for a five-minute walk in the woods. Walk, feel the crunch, smell the fragrances, try the different paths, and open your mouth to speak with God and open your ears to hear His answer.

SCRIPTURE

"A word was brought to me in secret; my ears caught a whisper of it."

JOB 4:12 (HCSB)

PRAYER

Thank you, Lord, that I can be certain that you believe in the "New Me" and that I can know you are walking with me as I explore new paths and directions in my life. Help me learn to speak to you boldly and listen in quietness as I begin to recognize your voice amidst the constant flow of thoughts going through my mind.

Waves of Peace

Was your day hectic or do you have a busy day planned for tomorrow? Are you a little stressed? If so, let's soften that stress by going "tripping" to the beach in your mind. If a favorite beach picture comes to mind, great…go there. If not, see yourself on a secluded stretch of a beach somewhere on a tropical isle. It's early, the sun is freshly up, and it's God-light kissing your face. You're walking in the soft sand, listening for the God-whispers of heaven. You are the only one there as the early morning waves roll in peacefully, one after another. The beach is surrounded by palm trees and a gentle breeze moves the palm fronds and ruffles your hair.

Wiggle your toes into the soft white sand…making yourself feel like a kid again. As you walk in the soft sand, you see the gulls weaving overhead and hear their calls. You find a big boulder or sand dune, climb up on the top and just watch the waves. See how

God's constancy is like the waves.

they keep rolling in, one on top of another…then fading back into the deep to return again. God's constancy is like the waves; He never walks away from you, but your busyness can cause Him to seem far away. You are reminded of the vastness of the seas and the order of the tides and God's desire to keep coming back to you. God whispers in your ear to breathe deeply and evenly. As you smell the salty air, you close your eyes and listen to the soothing sounds of the waves and of the gulls. Your stress is draining away as you embrace the peace of God. Give your worries for the day to Him. Make a decision to just take one minute of the day at a time. Decide to look for and find reasons to be thankful for the good things in your life. Have you ever read the poem about seeing one set of footprints in the sand and realize that it's Jesus who is carrying you? No matter what happens, keep your arms around His neck, relax in peace as, together, you continue your walk down the beach.

Decide to look for and find reasons to be thankful for the good things in your life.

Reflection...

_____

_____

_____

_____

_____

Flight of Fancy

Now take these mind pictures, close your eyes and imagine yourself in this small spot of paradise. Just sit, listen to the waves, feel the peace of God roll over you with each wave you see brushing the shore. Breathe deeply and relax for these few moments before you jump into the day, or before you slip quietly into a peaceful sleep this evening. Really imagine yourself there on the beach and feel, see, and smell as you relax into Jesus. Take these 5 minutes and express to Jesus what you are thinking and feeling, then wait for Him to whisper an answer. No sun-screen needed!

SCRIPTURE

"He stilled the storm to a murmur, and the waves of the sea were hushed. They rejoiced when the waves grew quiet. Then He guided them to the harbor they long for."

PSALM 107:29-30 (HCSB)

PRAYER

Thank you, Papa God, for bringing me to this place of peace and relaxation for a few moments…even if only in my imagination!

Twittering with Jesus

*I*sn't it wonderful to listen to the birds of spring returning to our trees from their winter hiatus? Just this morning, I was watching two cardinals that are obviously a couple. The Lord created them so beautiful with a recognizable chirp and warble…and I realized that what I thought was a mockingbird sound was really the sound of the cardinals. They were flitting from tree to tree and branch to branch, constantly "twittering" to each other about what they were thinking!

Apparently, that's what happens on Twitter…people are constantly sharing their thoughts, whether deep or superficial. People seem to have a need to communicate with those they love, and all those with whom they share some level of relationship. Jesus would really love to be part of your Twitter circle of communication.

He loves to listen to your thoughts, questions, ramblings, and whatever you want to share with Him. But He also wants to be able to "twitter" back to you. He wants to answer your questions and speak into your life. The problem is we often don't stay still long enough to listen for His voice, to recognize the sound of His voice. Just as the birds in an aviary recognize the sound of birds of like kind, Jesus recognizes your voice because you are made in His image and are like Him.

God's Word says He is aware of the birds and cares for their every need, and how much more He wants to care for you. But He is waiting for you to invite Him into your space. As you begin to find some time for silence, God will speak into your mind and heart. Soon you'll recognize if what you are thinking is from God, yourself, or the enemy. It takes some practice, but soon you'll feel confident in hearing His voice.

As you begin to find some time for silence,
God will speak into your mind and heart.

Reflection...

_____

_____

_____

_____

_____

Flight of Fancy

Now take your five minutes of flight, close your eyes and picture your-self in an aviary full of beautiful, gorgeous birds of every sound and color. Remember, God crafted them all just as He has crafted you. Even in the midst of the birds twittering in musical madness, if your "Father" stepped into the aviary and called out your name, you would hear Him and recognize His voice. Practice listening for the voice of Jesus even amidst the cacophony of your daily life.

SCRIPTURE

"To Him the doorkeeper opens, and the sheep hear His voice; and He calls His own sheep by name and leads them out. And when He brings out His own sheep, He goes before them; and the sheep follow Him, for they know His voice... My sheep hear My voice, and I know them, and they follow Me."

JOHN 10:3-4, 27 (NKJV)

PRAYER

Lord, give me the desire to twitter and talk with You even more than I do with others. Thank You that You want to hear from me and know my thoughts and ramblings. Thanks for being my sounding board, Jesus, and for knowing my voice. Help me learn to know Yours the moment I hear You speak!

Laughing into Joy

*D*o you ever picture God and Jesus laughing, not just a little smile but really sharing a big belly laugh where your eyes begin to water and your tummy muscles hurt? What…you don't think They ever laugh? Don't keep Them locked in a box of sternness or moroseness; sometimes, I think They laugh at their creations! You have to admit, sometimes we can be pretty crazy and tell funny jokes and stories. And think about all the animals They created…the giraffe…I'll bet Their first draft of the giraffe made Them laugh out loud! When I found this photo of the giraffe on the facing page he made me laugh!

Do you ever picture God and Jesus laughing…

I'm sure you've seen videos of little babies laughing. What an infectious sound and soon you find yourself laughing along and wanting to watch the video again and again. In my family, we sometimes say we "get our tickle box turned over"…you just can't seem to stop laughing.

You may be thinking…*Oh, how I wish I had something to laugh about…the funds are low, my body isn't well, the kids are out of control, I have no time to relax*…and on and on. It's easy to fall into a pity party and I know that times can be tough. But I want to challenge you today to find at least one thing to laugh about. If nothing else, get someone to tickle you! Laughing lessens tension, burns calories, and has shown to have healing power! Plus, it will remind you to *choose* joy in your life. I believe joy is a choice, but I think many people believe joy is a feeling that we wait to happen *to* us.

Remember, the Lord made you and loves you and that in itself is reason for joy!

*In Your presence is fullness of joy;
at Your right hand are pleasures forevermore.*

— PSALM 16:11 NKJV

Reflection...

_____

_____

_____

_____

_____

Flight of Fancy

Now, get ready to close your eyes and picture Jesus and Papa God laughing together (probably at something They saw you do). What a beautiful picture that is. As you see this picture, think of times and things that make you smile or laugh out loud. Take a deep breath and relax. Make a decision that, no matter what you are facing, you have the power to choose joy for your life rather than live under a cloud of pity and sadness.

SCRIPTURE

"A cheerful heart is good medicine, but a broken spirit saps a person's strength." Also, Nehemiah 8:10 – "Do not sorrow, for the joy of the Lord is your strength."

PROVERBS 17:22 (NKJV)

PRAYER

Thank You for reminding me, Jesus, that I can choose joy even in difficult circumstances. Give me Your strength and new eyes today to see something that I can laugh about and be filled with Your Spirit of Joy.

Now Boarding

oday, we're going to dream about boarding an airplane for a real vacation. You're thinking, *I haven't been on a real vacation in such a long time!* Well, today is your lucky day. You're going on a "God-away"! Even when you can't actually "get away," you can always take a "God-away."

In just a few minutes, during your Flight of Fancy, you are going to board the plane with God. You are so excited because God has bought both of you first class tickets…no economy section on this trip! You are a little nervous because you don't know the destination…it's His secret! But God knows where you need to go at this moment in your life…safe with Him, in His care, and free from worry.

He leads you to your seat in first class…wow, it's like your own little cubby! God says, "Give me your baggage, I'll handle it for you." He disappears for a moment to get rid of the baggage you were dragging with you. He sits down next to you and says, "You just sit still with Me in peace right now and enjoy the trip. I'm going to remind you of all the times I've been with you and protected you and just loved you for who you are and how I made you. Remember, I'll always be your travel guide."

You begin to relax and lean your head on God's shoulder. You feel the stress draining away, you put your worries in a little bag and hand it to God who blows into the bag and the worries are gone! Soon, you see swaying palm trees out the window and blue, translucent water. You're there in spirit, if not actually in body. Imagine yourself in a hammock on a peaceful beach and enjoy the rest of your vacation. God brought you on this trip, so remember, He'll never leave you there alone!

Give and it will be given to you; good measure, pressed down, shaken together, and running over will be put into your lap.

— LUKE 6:38 NKJV

Reflection...

_____
_____
_____
_____
_____

Flight of Fancy

Now you've read the story, take your five minutes and get on that plane with God. Imagine all the details I wrote about above. Put your worries in God's bag and let Him blow them away. "Now boarding... God-Away Airlines." Three, two, one...go!

SCRIPTURE

"May the Lord be praised! Day after day He bears our burdens; God is our salvation."

PSALM 68:19 (HCSB)

PRAYER

God, I give You my worries and anxieties. Thank You, dear Lord, that You'll always be here to share my load and carry my burdens. Thank You that I can always lean into Your peace and love...and, Jesus, thank You that You always treat me as "first class"!

The Great Imaginator

I hope, at the very beginning of the book, you read the "Preface" where I gave you directions. I coined a new description of God as the great *Imaginator*. I like that, because not only did He bring His imagination to life by creating the world and you, He gave you an imagination too! Think about the "day" God decided He was going to create the world. He was lonely for *us*...for *you* and for *me*. That in itself should blow your mind! Did you ever think that God had to *imagine* what this world would look like before He began creating it? *Imagination became reality!*

So today, like each day, we're going to use our imagination again, but today, we're going to really step out of our comfort zone and create a new world for just today. During your Flight of Fancy in a few moments, you're going to imagine a whole new day for yourself. I want you to think about what your day would look like if you could do anything you wanted today except, of course, illegal or immoral things! I don't know what you face today or are expecting tomorrow — an angry boss, bratty kids, financial needs, unfulfilled expectations, etc. Today, you can let that go as a way of living in Jesus. With Jesus, all things are possible. Remember, what you imagine can become reality as Jesus shows you His ways of accomplishing your dreams.

Imagination became reality!

*Whatever the mind of man
can conceive (imagine) and believe,
it can achieve.*

— NAPOLEON HILL

Reflection...

_____

_____

_____

_____

_____

Flight of Fancy

Now take five minutes and close your eyes. Restructure your day or even your week or month...maybe even your life (but that may take more than five minutes!). Let yourself imagine what life would be like "if only" or "what if I could do this or that." Just maybe, Jesus will give you a thought or picture of how some of your imaginings could become reality! Remember, sometimes changing just one small thing can lift a burden or give you new perspective and make your reality a more joyful place to live.

SCRIPTURE

"For God may speak in one way, or in another, yet man does not perceive it. In a dream, in a vision of the night, when deep sleep falls upon men, while slumbering on their beds. Then He opens the ears of men, and seals their instruction."

JOB 33:14-16 (NKJV)

PRAYER

Lord, give me dreams and imagination to bring new hope into my heart and mind. Give me wisdom to understand what You want to show me!

Percolating

What a funny word…long ago associated with making coffee. That was before the days of espresso machines that *hissss* and *foooam* and *bub…bub…bubble*. Or there's your more normal coffeemaker where you can hear the drip-drip of the coffee as the delicious brown liquid goes through the filter. Now we even have the newer, as I call them, "pop and press" machines where you insert a small plastic holder of flavored coffee into the machine, press a handle or button, and whoosh…almost instantly, you have an individual cup of coffee meeting your own expectations! Isn't life great!

Is your mouth watering as you begin to smell and taste the coffee in your imagination? Maybe you're actually drinking a cup now as you read. But let's talk about percolating or filtering. Do you know that every thought you have is "colored" because it comes percolating through the filter of your experiences? You may have had a wonderful childhood and great parents, or you may have experienced heartache, hurt, and abuse growing up. Whatever you experienced has colored your worldview because it has become the mental filter through which you interpret everything you see and hear as you view your world. However, the miraculous thing is that, Jesus wants to give you a new filter. *Imagine* getting a new filter that keeps your current thoughts and feelings from having to go through a filter full of anger, hurt, abuse, abnormal expectations, and warped worldviews. *Imagine* having a filter that is shaped by Jesus and your thoughts have to process only through a clean, pure filter. In this case, your imagination can truly become reality!

Your outer world is a reflection of your inner world. If you change your thinking, you change your life.

— BRIAN TRACY

Reflection...

_____

_____

_____

_____

_____

Flight of Fancy

In your five minutes today, I invite you to let Jesus renew your filter. Close your eyes and look into your past. Find the areas that need to be cleaned. Then ask God to give you a new filter. Pray out loud and pray to break generational patterns of expectations, abuse, unworthiness, living in need, etc...whatever makes you see life as out of kilter and robs you of joy. Ask God to release into your mind and heart a new set of DVDS to play...don't rewind your old tapes. Imagine and ask and believe! God loves to give us new filters. Remember, as we discovered a few readings ago, you are a "*new you*." Don't try to put something new back into something old, dirty, and worn out. Have a great cup of coffee today!

SCRIPTURE

"And no one puts new wine into old wineskins. Otherwise, the skins burst, the wine spills out, and the skins are ruined. But they put new wine into fresh wineskins, and both are preserved."

MATTHEW 9:17 (HCSB)

PRAYER

Thank You, Jesus, for giving me a new filter to process my new life in You. Lord, I fling all the old tapes from my past to the foot of Your cross. There, they are erased and replaced with my new life in You!

God's Hues — Fall: One of God's Most Beautiful Seasons

Winter's cold and snow have chilled our bones,
We longed for Spring to free us from our homes.
Spring's renewal smells have long since gone
And changed to Summer's dusty green.
Dusty green and summer heat are tiresome
And we look for God to paint a brand new scene.

He's always watching, caring, for He knows
Our human need to break monotony of days.
So God begins to paint the dusty green
To orange, red & yellow and soon
He hears our praise!

What is more beautiful than the colors of Fall? Even though I live in Texas and Fall is sometimes brief or unnoticeable — perhaps you live in a tropical paradise and don't even experience Fall, still we've all seen pictures or

The world will see God's face in your countenance...

perhaps traveled to places and experienced the beauty of the landscape in the Fall. Our eyes are riveted by changing colors as the hardwood trees are transformed by the touch of the fingers of God's creative genius into cavalcades of color splashed across hills and up the mountainsides, down in the valleys, even just lining a road or driveway. You're seeing it in your mind as you read, aren't you? I am too. Aren't our imaginations wonderful? Our imaginations can take us to so many wonderful places. Today, I simply want you to bask in the wonder of God's ability to transform the natural and commonplace into breathtaking beauty beyond description. Not just the material world around us…but us…you and me! He wants to transform your spirit, who you are, into someone even more beautiful. The world will see God's face in your countenance and in your actions every day.

Reflection...

_____

_____

_____

_____

_____

Flight of Fancy

Now close your eyes and let God recolor and transform you. Let His peace flow into those areas of anxiety to soften your face and slow your heartbeat. Allow Jesus to repaint the dusty green of everyday into vibrant colors of new life in Him. Picture yourself on God's canvas and feel the tickle of His brushes as He gently and carefully paints the new you!

SCRIPTURE

"We all, with unveiled faces, are looking as in a mirror at the glory of the Lord and are being transformed into the same image from glory to glory; this is from the Lord who is the Spirit."

2 CORINTHIANS 3:18 (HCSB)

PRAYER

I praise You, Maker of the Universe, that You love me enough to transform me daily to reflect You more and more. Each day I will thank You for Your unending love and for repainting each day those small blemishes that the enemy seeks to put on me daily. Thank You that Your gentle brush strokes keep me moving from "glory to glory" by Your Spirit.

The Fragrance of a Rose

I know that, just from reading the title of today's message, your imagination is already remembering the fragrance of a rose you once smelled. Good for you! My husband and I have been doing mission work in Romania since 2003, working primarily with the worldwide Youth With A Mission (YWAM) organization. Many things and places there are very different from the United States, but God's fingers did not miss Romania. It is a beautiful country to see, especially when it's not winter when everything is white! But even then, the purity of white snow can be transformingly beautiful!

God wants to surprise you with suddenlies and moments of beauty.

Once when we were there teaching, we were walking down the dirt driveway toward the dusty, rough street that ran in front of the YWAM base house. In the front area of the base is a small orchard and the driveway was lined with a few rosebushes. Most of the roses blooming were the usual red color, somewhat past full bloom and looking worn. Even their smell was not so "rosy." I realized I was a little disappointed — my expectation of the roses was not met. I'm sure that you experience disappointments, even small ones, on a daily basis. But time goes on and we accept the disappointments as part of life. So, we keep on walking down our daily path.

We continued down the driveway when, *suddenly*, I saw it. At the very end of the driveway, I saw a small rosebush with a single rose. It was an exquisite peach-colored rose just opening from the bud stage. It was beautiful in its perfection…the picture of a perfect rose bud. I wanted to smell it but hesitated as I was afraid my expectation of discovering a completely perfect rose with a heavenly fragrance would not be met. Realizing I couldn't resist the urge, I bent down and took a gentle smell…ahhh…the aroma of God. It was the strong, sweet, expected smell of the rose. I smiled! Once again, I was reminded that God does not disappoint — I just need to stay on His path.

Look for moments of *suddenlies* in your day…for the rose among the thorns. God wants to surprise you with *suddenlies* and moments of beauty. You just need to be looking. Make it a habit to look each day with your God-eyes to find your treasure for the day. But what are *suddenlies*? I *imagine* they are unexpected magical moments. They may vary greatly by what you need — a lovely picture, a kind word, a smile of love or encouragement, a familiar smell or taste, or sound that evokes sweet memories, even your ability to be a *suddenly* in someone else's world! A *suddenly* is only limited by your **imagination**.

Reflection...

_____

_____

_____

_____

_____

Flight of Fancy

If you're beginning the day now, be determined to look for those *suddenly* moments today and use your God-eyes so you don't miss what God has in store for you. If you're reading just before bedtime, replay your last few days and find the moments that you didn't realize were your *suddenlies*. May you smell the fragrance of God in the simple things of life.

SCRIPTURE

"For we are to God the fragrance of Christ among those who are being saved and among those who are perishing."

2 CORINTHIANS 2:15 (NKJV)

PRAYER

Father God, help me to look for and recognize the suddenlies You put into my life each day. Forgive me for not concentrating on looking for those beautiful moments, thoughts, or pictures that You send me each day just to remind me that You are still with me.

DAY 11

Father of Lights

D o you remember the sweet and simple Christian chorus with the same name as the title of today's message? It was popular in the '80s or '90s. The chorus began, *"Father of lights, you delight in your children.... every good and perfect gift comes from you...."* Perhaps your memory was sparked when you read the title and are even now humming the tune with sweet memories. In this and the next devotion, we are going to talk about the beauty of light. I want you to remember a time when you experienced seeing some extraordinary lights. I'll help you with a list: the Aurora Borealis, a star-spangled sky on a moonless night, fireworks on the Fourth of July, a morning sunrise across the ocean, a fiery

...God created us to be lights to a hurting world...

sunset, a vibrant rainbow, joyful lights in the eyes of a child...even "lights" in a glowworm cave (more about this tomorrow!)...you get the idea.

We know that God created us to be lights to a hurting world, but I know that, some days, we feel like we can't shine at all. I want to challenge you today to not hide your light under a basket because you definitely have a light to share with the world around you. "Why?" you ask. "How do you know?" Because God created **you** with a special light to share in your circle of influence. I believe that light begets more light, not only physically but also emotionally. In a dark place, a single candle dispels the darkness around you physically. In a dark place in your mind, a single God-light thought can begin to move depression into hope. But you must make the first move to turn your light on!

41

Whether you think you can or
you think you can't, you're right.

— HENRY FORD

Reflection...

Festival of Lights @ Disneyland - way back
when they brought the Light Parade down Main Street.
Tomorrow Land as a young girl & walking into
Tomorrow Land w my family for the first time.
Light, bright, alive - Hope for a bright future.
Future, freedom, the music, the colors, the
energy - the Tiki Room - another place of
wonder for me...

Flight of Fancy

See yourself on a secluded beach sitting on a rock, waiting for the sun to rise across the water. Dawn is breaking and you wonder what the new day will bring. Soon you see shades of pink forming...the pink fades into pale yellow and, all around you, the area is waking up... you can now see the beauty of the flowers on the dunes and tiny crabs scrambling for cover. You watch in awe as you see rays of light fanning upward at the horizon as the sky turns more orange...then the emerging curve of the sun peeks over the horizon in a blaze of glory. (What's so wonderful about imagining is you don't have to worry about protecting your eyes!) There, once again, always faithful...the sun is rising to surround you with warmth today and give you opportunity to share your light abroad. Think of at least one thing you will do today (or tomorrow if you're reading this at bedtime) that will sprinkle some of God's light into another person's life. Now close your eyes and slip into this picture in your mind and stay there a few moments!

SCRIPTURE

"You are the light of the world. A city that is set on a hill cannot be hidden. Nor do they light a lamp and put it under a basket, but on a lampstand, and it gives light to all who are in the house. Let your light so shine before men, that they may see your good works and glorify your father in heaven."

MATTHEW 5:14-16 (NKJV)

PRAYER

Father, use me as Your God-light to shine Your light into my family, my school, my workplace, the grocery store, shopping mall...forgive me for allowing my daily burdens to become a basket that hides my light. Wherever I walk, let me leave footprints of You!

Magical Lights

Today, I'm going to tell you a true story about a type of light you've likely never experienced. The story in itself will make you see it all in your imagination. So join me for a longer than usual reading, but I think you'll love this unique experience.

Now, about that glowworm cave I mentioned in yesterday's devotion. Did you know such a thing exists? My son and his four precious kids (our grandkids!) visited New Zealand in 2013 where the locals told them they should visit the glowworm cave...not on the list of normal sight-seeing events. But always up for adventure, they found what they hoped was the path (but no direction signs!) off a small rural road in the middle of a sheep pasture. As they tentatively began to walk the pathway they'd discovered and hoped was the right way, they finally passed a father and daughter coming in the opposite direction who confirmed that they were on the right path.

My son, who just happens to plan for all possibilities when traveling, had packed headlamps for all five of them! They'd also been told they might get their feet a little wet. Finally, a sign pointed them to the opening of the cave. Indeed, their feet would get wet because they realized they would have to walk into the cave through a stream. The kids were ages seven, ten, fourteen, and sixteen but they totally trusted their father, so they began the trek into the darkness. They trod carefully in the water and over slippery rocks, thanking God for their headlamps. The farther they went into the cave and away from the light of the cave opening, they began to see little twinkles in their peripheral vision. Their headlamps were shining straight ahead of them. Our son, Chad, said to the children, "I think we're far enough in, let's turn off our headlamps." Suddenly, they realized that around them, the cave had "awakened" as they seemed to be surrounded by "lights." They said it was like they were floating in the heavens, in a magical world encircled by heavenly stars…yet it was hundreds of glowworms. At one point, they walked further into the cave and came to a pool of water that was absolutely calm. Then it seemed they were totally suspended in the lights of heaven above and below from the reflection of the pool. They began to sing some praise songs and thank God for their amazing experience. The children wouldn't have experienced this if not for their belief that there is indeed light in the darkness and trusted to follow their father.

This young family was acquainted with darkness, our son having lost his wife — and the kids, their mother — to breast cancer four-and-a-half months before this trip. There are things we can glean from this story. We often keep our focus straight ahead where we can see some light, yet sometimes, we catch a glimpse of lights in our periphery. However, many of us tend to keep pointed in the same direction so as not to get off the main path. But the Lord has so many lights He wants to show us if we're not afraid to look past the darkness in our lives. He wants us to trust and follow Him on the path He intends for us.

Besides a wonderful story to read, imagine yourself being with them. They had truly walked through the "valley of the shadow of death" for fifteen months, but they all kept their eyes focused on Jesus — the healer, the provider, the protector, and the Father of Lights! They've chosen not to dwell in the dark places, but instead begin to look for new lights to shine into their lives and see what the Lord has planned for them. Every one of his amazing children and our son have eyes alight with joy and optimism as they greet each new day. Some days are still hard, but they all **choose** to look for the day's opportunity to shine for Jesus.

Reflection…

_____

_____

_____

_____

_____

Flight of Fancy

Now I want you to take five minutes and walk through the glowworm cave and see the lights of these magical little creatures God has created. Listen for God's sweet voice to call out to you as you choose to explore a new path. He will call you to look carefully as you walk so you don't wander down a wrong path. He wants you to discover new lights in your life. So, trust Him to surround you with His light as He leads you on in His love. Now keep your eyes closed and make the trek through the stream into the darkness. Then turn off your headlamp, see the glowworms, and listen for His voice in the magical stillness of the cave.

SCRIPTURE

"For with You is the fountain of life; In Your light we see light."

PSALM 36:9 (NKJV)

PRAYER

Who but You, Master Creator, would think to create a tiny creature like a glowworm? They must be cousins to the "lightning bugs" we have in the South in the United States. Your desire is to create light in the darkness. Father, use me to cast the glow of Your light in my circle of influence.

Note: The photo for today's reading was actually taken in a glowworm cave in New Zealand.

Clouds

*I*magine this:

God woke up this morning, lifted His hands up high over His head, and had a good stretch and a wake-up yawn. (I know, I know, God never sleeps but stay with me!) He peeked out the window of heaven and a mischievous smile spread across His face. Finding Jesus already awake, He said, "Hey, Son, look out the window and tell me what you see."

Jesus looked out with a big smile and said, "A gorgeous blue sky, totally perfect!"

God said, "Yes, but it looks a little plain… do you want to play 'cloud-blowing' with me and open the doors to heaven a little wider today?"

He wants you to remember that They know your name in Heaven….

For an answer, they both run toward the stack of drinking straws in their heavenly kitchen and each grab one. Now, bear with me…I see both of them as really ginormous so, of course, their straws are sizeable…like you could blow a Volkswagen Beetle through them! But where do they blow? They reach into a huge bucket of names and, amazingly, they pick out your name and your little part of the world. They discuss you by name and decide that today needs to be a special day for you to imagine and just think of fun things. So they begin to blow special clouds through their straws right into your area. Not the rainy type…oh no! These are the fabulous white, puffy, cotton-ball type that shift and change shape and patterns slowly as you gaze at them.

Remember when you were a kid and you used to lie in the grass and stare up at the clouds? You would often "see" different things in the clouds and think, *I see a dragon* or *there's a bulldog* or *that one looks like Abraham Lincoln*.... What fun it was to just relax, lying back on the grass, watching the cloud pictures you see morphing into something new as the minutes passed. God wants **you**, _____ (fill in your name), to be a kid again for a few moments. You have to admit it's been fun picturing God and Jesus having a cloud-blowing contest just for you!

Reflection...

_____

_____

_____

_____

_____

Flight of Fancy

Now take five minutes and lie back if possible and see yourself on a grassy hill under the shadow of a huge tree that protects you from the sun, but doesn't obstruct your view of the sky. Watch the clouds and let God show you some things in the clouds that make you giggle, be awed, or bring back a sweet memory. Now breathe slowly and deeply and relax. This is a moment for you to realize how much God loves you just because you're you. He wants you to remember that They know your name in heaven and are always looking for ways to say, "We love you…relax in this moment…everything is under control."

SCRIPTURE

"Do you understand how He moves the clouds with wonderful perfection and skill?"

Job 37:16 (NLT)

PRAYER

Oh, Papa God, thank You for reminding me of happy times sky gazing and seeing cloud paintings! And You know what, God? Even as an adult, I still look for pictures in the sky to share with those I'm with when we're going on a long drive or when we're out camping or when I'm just out alone sky gazing! Thank You for blowing clouds my way! I love You, Papa God! Oh look, Papa! That one looks just like a Volkswagen Beetle!

Waterfalls

I've never been to Niagara Falls but have seen photos and watched videos and heard the deafening sounds of the water. However, I have been to Hawaii and seen some spectacular waterfalls there, and in Yosemite National Park also. Maybe you can picture in your mind a waterfall you've visited. Do you remember a huge waterfall or is it a tiny one in a little protected stream, falling in a pattern down four or five small rocks into a gently swirling pool? The power of the water always strikes awe into my soul. Whether it's a big or small waterfall, the waterfall has the power to move things.

Today I want you to see your Abba Father, your Papa God, as a waterfall. One thing about water is that it is always wet! When you are near it, sometimes you get sprayed or you run through a waterfall in glee just to feel it

...His waterfall for you today is His never ending love!

pouring over you. Your Father God wants you to know that His waterfall for you today is His never-ending love! He always wants you to remember that His love, like water, washes things clean and makes them sparkle.

If you're feeling a little covered by the cares of the world around you, remember God is your waterfall, so…

As the Father loved Me,
I also have loved you; abide in My love

— JOHN 15:9 NKJV

Reflection...

_____

_____

_____

_____

_____

Flight of Fancy

Read this, then put yourself into this picture I'm painting as you read… and stay there for a couple of minutes with Jesus. There is a secluded little beach with a large cliff behind it and, unbelievably, there is a waterfall pouring forth from the foliage on top of the cliff. It's streaming down forty feet into the wet sand and running into the surf. It's like an oasis in the desert. You are hot and thirsty and wishing for respite from the sun's heat. You approach and see that, inside the waterfall, stands a brilliant figure beckoning you to come in. You think you're losing your mind, but the scene is irresistible. You walk in and realize you're with Jesus when He takes your hand and smiles. He calls you by name and says, "_____ (your name), this is My power pouring over you, filling you with strength, healing, joy, peace, and trust. It is washing away all of the dust of the day that you feel covered in. Know that you can stay here with Me as long or as often as you wish. I'll always be here. Oh yes, and while you're here, take a sip or two of My water and you'll be refreshed from the inside out." Now keep this image in your head as you're off to work or tuck yourself into bed!

SCRIPTURE

"As the deer longs for streams of water, so I long for you, O God."

PSALM 42:1 (NLT)

PRAYER

Lord, You are my waterfall to wash me daily in Your love. Help me stay close enough to You, so that I never feel less of You than the droplets of Your spray. But Father, let me seek not only Your droplets; let me feel immersed in the endless refreshment of Your living water.

Rainbows

A h, rainbows! Now here is something I know everyone can imagine because most people have actually seen one! Isn't it interesting that almost every time you see one — whether it's faint and only partial or brilliant and the arches stretch from the ground at point A to the ground at point B where the *pot of gold* is — we exclaim out loud in an excited voice, "Oh, look over there…see the rainbow!" It just seems to bring forth joy from us as we stare in wonder and awe at what God creates. I think many of us are reminded of God's promise regarding the rainbow.

Let me remember the pot of gold filled with Your promises waiting for me…

Today, I want you to imagine a gorgeous, deeply colored, gigantic rainbow overarching your home. You can see it from beginning to end. Then picture God telling you to walk to where one side of the rainbow ends and find that *pot of gold*. That *pot of gold* is filled with God's promises to you from His Word. Do a little study when you have time and find all the promises of God to us in His Word!

Better than gold, more wonderful than fame and fortune, are the promises of God.

For all the promises of God are Yes and
Amen in Him, to the glory of God through us.

— II Cor. 1:20 NKJV

Reflection...

_____

_____

_____

_____

_____

Flight of Fancy

Now, read below then close your eyes and put yourself in the rainbow picture. Relax and start walking to the end of the rainbow; it's not too far. There, now you see the pot of shining gold. It's so bright it's almost blinding. You can hear God whispering in the stillness, "Here, my child...sit and read my promises to you." The pot is filled with tiny golden scrolls tied with golden ribbon. As you take one in your hand, you feel a warmth spread over you as you carefully open it and read God's words to you. The whisper continues, "Know that you are never alone. Lean on my promises."

SCRIPTURE

"Because of His glory and excellence, He has given us great and precious promises. These are the promises that enable you to share his divine nature and escape the world's corruption caused by human desires."

2 PETER 1:4 (NLT)

PRAYER

Father God, remind me to see the rainbow over my home every day, even if it is in my imagination! Let me remember the pot of gold filled with Your promises waiting for me to claim. Your promises are here for the taking and Your blessings are countless. Remind me to count those blessings each day! You are so wonderful, Lord!

Raindrops

o you remember smelling the raindrops coming? At the end of a long, dry, hot summer, you are longing for the cooling rain. The grass is all brown and dust is everywhere. Can you see it? You're sitting outside on the front steps of an old farmhouse saying, "God, we need some rain!" Then you see a cloud in the distance and it's coming your way, gathering strength as it comes. Then, suddenly, you smell the moisture and hear the first plops of raindrops. You see the tiny indentations of the drops in the dry dirt. That's when you really

...smell the peace of His presence.

begin to smell the raindrops. After they hit the dirt, it changes the composition and sets off a distinct smell that makes you smile. Ah, relief! It's a unique smell — raindrops.

I read a beautiful story once about a little boy who told his mother that the raindrops smelled like God. She laughed and asked, "What made you think of that?" He said he'd been talking to his little sister, Sara, the last time it rained and Sara asked him, "Do you remember?"

He replied, "Remember what?"

Sara said, "Before I was born I remember that God always smelled like fresh rain when He hugged me."

The mother found herself unable to speak as "rain drops" pooled in her eyes.

So, when you feel surrounded by rain clouds in your life, remember that God is in them and will never leave you…and smell the peace of His presence.

Before I was born
I remember that God
always smelled like fresh rain
when He hugged me.

Reflection...

_____
_____
_____
_____
_____

Flight of Fancy

Now, picture yourself on those porch steps and remember a time when it rained and you could actually smell the drops as they broke the dry spell. Thank God for being in the midst of the rain and realize that rain actually refreshes as it makes things new and produces growth. Next, picture flowers growing up around you as if in time-lapse photography. Your dry spell will soon be changed into a beautiful landscape with the smell of "God-drops" all around you. Thank Jesus for helping you see the changes coming!

SCRIPTURE

"Let us strive to know the LORD. His appearance is as sure as the dawn. He will come to us like the rain, like the spring showers that water the land."

HOSEA 6:3 (HCSB)

PRAYER

Oh God, thank You for changing my view of rain. Rain doesn't always bring gloom and sadness. No, it brings refreshment and renewal. I can't wait until the next rain, Lord, as I want to smell Your "after-shave" named "God-Drops." I'll remind my friends it can be found in their local yards made exclusively by Masterpiece Fragrances! Papa God, You make me smile!

Soaring with Jesus

I'll bet you, like me and probably like most others, have — at one time or another — turned our heads skyward and watched a hawk gracefully flap its wings, catch an updraft, and soar along...up and down...around and back and thought to yourself, *How cool to be able to fly and feel the wind beneath me!*

Today, we're going to be part of the class called **Beginner Flying 101**. No special skills required, no perfect vision needed, just a desire to fly and feel the freedom it brings. Supplies to bring: your imagination. Instructor: Jesus!

You may have seen movies that show large creatures from the "good side" swoop in at the last moment, just before the good guys fall off a cliff or are about to get skewered by the bad guys. The creatures snatch the good guys out of harm's way with their claws or catch them on their backs as they are falling toward the ground below the cliff. Imagine the good guys' sighs of relief. They are safe...they've been rescued by the wings of goodness!

Our relationship with Jesus is like that. Many times in our lives, we go through circumstances where we may feel like we're about to be overcome by the bad guys. Sometimes, even little things can make us afraid and we might face uncertainties many times a day. I want to challenge you today to walk in certainty that Jesus will catch you if you fall. He will rescue you and give you rest. Yes, we usually have to go through the consequences of our choices, or live with the trials that come from living in a fallen world. But Jesus will always be there.

Or maybe, something wonderful just happened to you and, out of sheer joy, you want to soar with Jesus...go ahead, soar away!

...take the step and fall into the softness of Love's power to save

Reflection...

_____

_____

_____

_____

_____

Flight of Fancy

Okay, now read through the guided imagery below, then close the book and your eyes and do the actions I will paint in your imagination. Picture yourself on a high mountain precipice, ready to burst into song from joy or crying out to Jesus for rescue. Now, look into the distance and see a beautiful winged creature zooming toward you. You know your choices are to jump on or duck as it swoops by. The Beautiful One is now close enough for you to see its face…glorious love pours from the eyes and it whispers into the wind, "Don't be afraid, I will slow down so that you have only to step onto my back. Let me carry you away."

Then, it's there and it pauses…you take the step and fall into the softness of Love's power to save. There is an indention like a little bed with handles on both sides near the neck. You lie down and grab hold. Love looks back at you and says, "Hold on, here we go!" Amazingly, you do not feel like you've been thrown into a wind tunnel, but a warm breeze blows across you as you soar in the arms of love. The wind joins in your joyful thanksgiving and blows away the fears you are facing. You relax in the pure rest of being held up by the love of Jesus. Now, take five minutes and soar with Him!

PS: You can "jump and soar" anytime or any place just for a fun "pick-me-up." It's like a free energy boost anytime and no calories!

SCRIPTURE

"But those who trust in the LORD will find new strength. They will soar high on wings like eagles. They will run and not grow weary. They will walk and not faint."

ISAIAH 40:31 (NLT)

PRAYER

Oh Lord, how I want to soar with You! Give me the courage to step out and fall into Your love's power to save. Thank you, Lord, that as I trust You more, You will renew my strength!

Life Under the Tree

There it is, the gate of entry. I didn't expect it to be so whimsical. Why, it's made of crystal and reflects the myriad of colors from the garden inside. I touch it gently with my hand and it's cool and smooth and shaped like an undulating ribbon across the top. The gate latch is pure gold. I open it and slowly walk in. There is no sound except the birds singing and a slight breeze whispering in the leaves of the plants. I'm excited and expectant as God invited me to join Him anywhere I wanted to picture in my mind. So, here I am in the Garden of Eden. Are you with me as you read? Come on! Our Abba is waiting for us!

Unbelievable…magnificent…it's hard to envision such beauty. The flowers are brilliant! They're in colors I recognize, yet different. Yes, there are reds, greens, blues,

I'm overwhelmed by His encompassing love and acceptance of me.

pinks, peach, lavender, purple, and more…but the hues are more intense than normal. The colors almost seem to send out waves of current that move your heart. And the fragrances... gentle and citrus here…intense and sweet there. There are paths to wander everywhere and discover new exotic plants in fabulous shapes and sizes. I keep walking until, suddenly, I stop and gasp. There in the center is the most magical, enormous tree I've ever seen. The green of the leaves fairly pulses…and the fruit hanging in profusion from the branches is a feast for the senses. I realize that I'm looking at the Tree of Life…and God says this is the one we can eat from freely! Amazing, this gift!

I quickly sink down on a small, sparkling glass bench to gaze at the beauty and soon I feel the presence of God surrounding me. I say, "Dear Papa God, you made all this for me?" He replies, "Yes, my child, it's yours for the taking…as much as you want…anytime…just choose out of your love for Me, for I've made this out of My love for you. Each fruit is a gift I want to give you. Now go and stand under the tree."

I walk slowly through the soft grass until I'm under the canopy of The Tree of Life. I have goose bumps all over! Then, soft music fills the air and leaves begin to gently fall from the tree — being replaced immediately — and they fall over and around me, softly brushing my body from head to toe. With each touch of a leaf, I feel love pouring in…refreshing me, cleansing me, and filling me with pure joy. Then I hear God whisper, "Choose some fruit." I pick a beautiful cluster of red grapes and, as I bite into one, I hear the words, "This gift represents the covenant of blood spilled for our unique and personal relationship. Eat it and make a covenant with Me."

As I begin to realize the wonder of my relationship with God, Jesus, and the Holy Spirit, I understand that each fruit I eat represents another gift for me to accept and learn to grow into. More gifts than I can name are hanging on the tree — love, joy, peace, patience, kindness, forgiveness, generosity, healing, authority, and more. I begin darting from gift to gift, then I see God pointing for me to look on the ground at the base of the tree. There are colorful flags waving. "Yes," He says, "take them home also. They are freedom flags." I began collecting the flags and each has a message: "Accept freedom from fear," "Freedom from anxiety," "Freedom from perfectionism," "Freedom from bitterness," "Freedom from lack," "Freedom from comparison," "Embrace forgiveness," and on and on. I see God watching me and He's laughing in delight, so thrilled that one of His children has come to His garden to meet with Him and take all the gifts He wants to give.

I'm overwhelmed by His encompassing love and acceptance of me. I gather my gifts and put them in a small wagon, beautifully painted to match the flowers He has placed nearby. I walk back through the garden to the gate and leave, quietly, closing it behind me. But I know it's not goodbye but "until later," I'll be back to fill my wagon once again.

Flight of Fancy

Wow, that was a little longer walk in the imagination, but I feel breathless, do you? Now, I want you to take five minutes, close your eyes and go into the garden by yourself, meet with God on the sparkling glass bench. Wait to hear what He wants to say to you about how much He loves you…then go stand under the Tree of Life and let it rain gifts down on you. Choose the gifts you need for today, or tomorrow, then rest in His love.

SCRIPTURE

"So if you sinful people know how to give good gifts to your children, how much more will your heavenly Father give good gifts to those who ask Him."

MATTHEW 7:11 (NLT)

PRAYER

Oh Father, I can only bow in thanks for Your gifts to me, Your child whom You love completely.

Twinkle, Twinkle Little Star

Stars, such a mystery and such a wondrous sight. I'm imagining that you may have had the opportunity to be away from the city lights and into an area void of artificial lighting…and it's a night when the moon is not shining. It's a dark, dark night but the heavenlies are gorgeous, like diamonds shaken from a bag onto black velvet, alive in the Milky Way and constellations. Thousands, millions, beyond counting are the number of stars, besides the bright planets of which we sometimes catch a glimpse. Just think, God made them all and was pleased with His handiwork.

Like He fashioned the stars, He fashioned you.

Like He fashioned the stars, He fashioned you. You are a glimmering star in His sight, created with many facets. He holds His breath to see what you will do with all the gifts and talents He has put into you. Will you discover some of those facets or believe the lie of the enemy that you have not much worth? You will always be a shining star in His sight. You have only to push aside the lies surrounding you and step into who you really are!

God knows your name!
You have a special place in His heart
that only you can fill.

Reflection...

_____
_____
_____
_____
_____

Flight of Fancy

If possible, go outside or look out your window if you can see the sky. Or, if you're reading this in the daytime or you're in bed, just close your eyes and imagine you are on a mountain top surrounded by millions of twinkling stars. Take your finger and trace your name among the stars and then remember…God knows your name! He sees you and, as you trace your name among the stars, He is tracing your name across His heart. You have a special place in His heart that only you can fill. Never believe the lies of the enemy who tries to convince you that you are not worthy of God's love. Stay in your imagination for a few minutes and enjoy life among the stars. Remember, He did it all for love…He did it all for you.

SCRIPTURE

"For I know the plans I have for you," says the LORD. "They are plans for good and not for disaster, to give you a future and a hope."

JEREMIAH 29:11 (NLT)

PRAYER

Lord, I bow before You in thanks that You did it all for me. It's hard to believe, yet I must…that You know my name! You created me special, one of a kind. Lord, lead me into the plans You have for me and that I, in turn, may help others realize the loveliness of their creation by Your hand…beautifully unique and painted in Your glory.

Baby's Breath

*H*ave you ever, at one time or another, held a newborn baby within its first month of life. There is something so precious and innocent in that small bundle. I hope you had the pleasure of snuggling that tiny one into your neck, or nuzzling the tiny face with your nose, smelling the newness of him or her. If, by chance, the baby yawned or even let out a small cry and you were close enough, you could smell the sweetness of the baby's breath. It is unique and yet, every newborn I've had the privilege of being so close to that I could smell their breath… every baby's breath had that same unique, sweet smell.

The Bible says God breathes into us the breath of life and it dawned on me that, maybe, the baby's breath we smell is the aroma of God that is *leftover* from God's breath! How astounding is that! God's creation of a living, tiny baby is surely the most magical of miracles! It is a living work of art and love incarnate. How much we are loved by God that He designs each of us uniquely, then breathes into us His breath of life. The slate is clean and new; how will this one show their love for God through their life?

Thank you, Lord, for seeing me as beautiful

Life is not measured by the number of breaths we take, but by the moments that take our breath away.

— MAYA ANGELOU

Reflection...

_____
_____
_____
_____
_____

Flight of Fancy

Okay, this is really going to stretch your imagination, but I want you to close your eyes and imagine yourself just as you draw your first breath as a newborn baby. God is there. I want you to imagine that you can feel His gentle fingers on your tiny face as He's giving you a hello kiss. He gently breathes into you the breath of life that fills your lungs and sets off the chain of events in your body that allows you to begin breathing air instead of liquid...what a miracle! In that one act of utter love, remember how much God loved you then...and still loves you *now*, no matter what circumstances you are in. God is all about clean slates and new beginnings. It only takes a "turning" and asking for forgiveness and, believe me, God's in the forgiveness business! On the other hand, if you're feeling confident in your relationship with Father, praise God and just revel in His breath in your life!

Future Flight of Fancy

Now, don't become a "stalker," but be on the lookout for a newborn baby of a friend or relative that you might be able to hold closely with the parent's permission. Take a whiff of that little one's breath and smell the breath of God. Remember, you and I all started with that breath in us too. Let's try to follow God in such a way that we will end our days with God's aroma in us and around us.

SCRIPTURE

"Then the LORD God formed the man from the dust of the ground and breathed into his nostrils the breath of life, and the man became a living being."

GENESIS 2:7 (NIV)

PRAYER

Precious Jesus, my Creator...how I thank You for fashioning me gently with Your fingers until You said, "Ah, now that's it...this one is just as I imagined...beautiful!" Thank You, Lord, for seeing me as beautiful when I so often disparage myself. Let me learn to live in the thoughts You have of me, not in how I see myself! Thank you for a new day each day! Remind me to breathe in Your aroma as I begin each day.

Sound of Silence

I think that sound and the ability to hear is one of God's greatest gifts, along with having eyes to see. In our world today, we are inundated with "noise" all around us. Many, young people especially, can hardly function unless they have earbuds in and something playing through their minds. Work places and stores have music playing in the background. It seems that many people are uncomfortable in an actual quiet place with no artificial sounds playing. But I believe God longs for us to find a quiet place to meet with Him…away from distractions…even from wonderful Christian music!

Count the blessings of the sounds of silence…

This may be hard, but I want you to try to imagine what God's voice will sound like when He speaks to you. There are a few voices I bet you have heard on TV or in movies that just catch your fancy, and it makes you feel good just to hear that person speak. Try to find a voice to recognize and make it your "go-to" voice when you find that special place to meet with God. If you are one of those always "plugged-in" people, today I want to challenge you to unplug and find a quiet spot, even if just for a few minutes, and talk to God and wait for Him to speak with you!

Watch your thoughts; they become words.
Watch your words; they become actions.
Watch your actions; they become habits.
Watch your habits; they become character.
Watch your character; it becomes your destiny

— FRANK OUTLAW

Reflection...

_____

_____

_____

_____

_____

Flight of Fancy

Whether you are getting tucked into bed or having your last few minutes of bedhead before starting your day, unplug all your portable electronics and *listen* to the silence. It has a *sound*...it's the sound of your surroundings. But wherever you are, don't despair that you aren't on a mountain top in the woods where you can find a more naturally silent environment. I want you to appreciate the little sounds of your home...the whirring motor of your refrigerator, the sound of your heating or AC unit coming on or cutting off; the sound of life around you...the sound your sheets make when you get up or lie down, the tic and the tock of your bedside clock. It's amazing when you learn to appreciate that God gives you many sounds to remind you how blessed you are by Him. Today, count your many big and little blessings in the sounds of silence!

SCRIPTURE

"Be still, and know that I am God."

PSALM 46:10 (NKJV)

PRAYER

Lord, I thank You that I have been reminded to listen to the sounds of silence so I can hear You. Forgive me, Lord, for getting so comfortable with earbuds and manmade sounds that it has become a habit. Lord, I want to learn to count the blessings of the sounds of silence that surround me so I can hear Your voice and praise You for those big and little blessings that are often hidden by other noise. Help me, Lord, as I begin to walk in this new path!

Granddaddy's House...
Love Extended

This imagination book is filled with love from cover to cover in many different fashions. Today, we're going to imagine love extended... beyond your central core family. I've mentioned before that you may not have had the most loving, caring core family or extended family. Maybe you didn't know your grandparents well or at all. So today, I'm letting you borrow mine! Come with me as you experience "love...extended!"

We kids were so excited to be going to Granddaddy and Grandmama's house thirty miles away. Traveling thirty miles today is done in the blink of an eye, but when I was a kid, it seemed to take forever! At last, we

He's always waiting for you with His arms wide open...

turn left on the final gravel road and pass Uncle Dee's house, knowing that Granddaddy's house is just a little farther down the road. Ah, at last, we turn into the little half-circle drive cut into the grass in front of the picket fence. Yep, like always, Granddaddy is sitting on the front porch with his old, stained felt hat on; his feet propped up on the rail and a cigar in one side of his mouth. (He looks a little grumpy because he always hates waiting for us to show up!) But before we can even get the car doors open, he is at the gate with arms wide open, smiling and giving welcome hugs. Then here comes Grandmama out the screen door, wearing her always present apron saying, "COME ON IN, Y'ALL. ARE YOU HUNGRY?" We kids never worried that Grandmama's cookie jar would be empty or that they had run out of RC Cola. (Popular before Coca-Cola ruled the world!) Once there, we stepped into a world of welcoming, accepting love and fun!

Living out in the country, they had the "grandkid horse" to ride and eggs to gather in the chicken house; watching Granddaddy milk the cows in the milk barn, driving the tractor in the corn field and gathering corn to toss in the small trailer pulled behind the tractor, drinking water from the community dipper at the windmill, and so much more. I never remember my Granddaddy being upset or angry with any of us grandkids. He was fun, a big tease, and everyone loved him. He used to embarrass Grandmama by giving her a hug or kiss on the cheek in front of us and she'd turn bright red!

We never had to wonder if they loved us. Love surrounded them and we felt covered in the security of that unconditional love. God is like that… His love is extended through His core family, Jesus, and the Holy Spirit. We can be sure, if we have asked Jesus into our hearts, that we are also covered and secure in Their love of us and that we belong to that wonderful family of God!

** "This photo for today's reading is the author's actual granddaddy impatiently waiting for the arrival of his children and grandchildren."

Reflection...

_____

_____

_____

_____

_____

Flight of Fancy

Now that you've pictured my grandparents' house in the country, I want you to take a little "field trip" in your imagination. See yourself driving up to the gate and feel enveloped in Granddaddy's love. Visit the dining room and find Grandmama's big glass cookie jar and have a cookie and some RC Cola. Then decide what activity you want to do and have at it! Let your mind go and paint a story of yourself as a child having a wonderful day in the country in Texas. After you get tired, go into the dairy barn and ask Granddaddy to get one of the watermelons cooling in the milk coolers. Can you taste the sweetness? What a glorious day. Now, go in their guest bedroom, lie across the bed, and look out the open window. Listen…no beeps, dings of phones or tablets, no taps of keyboards…just the buzzing of a passing bee, the chirps of birds, clucking of chickens…and the smell of hay in the barn, flowers, cows in the pen, and baking cookies in the kitchen! Thank God that He loves you even more than Granddaddy and Grandmama. Remember that He calls us to be like little children and come running to Him knowing He's always waiting for you with His arms wide open and "treats" to give us!

SCRIPTURE

"I will establish My covenant as an everlasting covenant between me and you and your descendants after you for the generations to come, to be your God and the God of your descendants after you."

GENESIS 17:7 (NIV)

PRAYER

Thank you, Father God, that You welcomed me into Your core family when I accepted Jesus into my heart. How wonderful to know that my name is written in Your book of descendants. And Lord, I praise You for my family here, both biological and spiritual, who surround me with love and encouragement.

Passion

Have you ever seen passion flowers up close? They are magnificent and have parts that will remind you of a crown fit for a king…King Jesus! The main color is bluish purple…a royal color. Did you ever think about the fact that the God of the universe is passionate about *you?* Now don't say, "Oh no. Not me! I'm not good enough for God to feel that way toward me."

Do you have something in your life that you are passionate about? Or do you know someone who is very passionate about something? How do you act or how do they act?

You are always on His mind.

You'd probably find yourself thinking about your passion all the time, be it a person, a thing, or a situation you are involved in. It's always on your mind. You're wondering how you can be more helpful, how you can show more care and concern, how you can protect what you are passionate about from harm.

God feels passionate about you. You are always on His mind. He is always waiting and watching for you to turn to Him and seek to relate to Him more fully. He wants the best for you and is rooting for you to make the right decisions every day. God gives us free will to make choices in our lives and, in those choices, we must live with the consequences and circumstances surrounding any given choice we make. That way of life came with "The Fall" in the Garden of Eden in the beginning. However, always remember that you can be certain of God's love. It's like a bubbling wellspring of water that never runs out, and He covers you completely each day in the water of His love.

I am God's masterpiece. He created me anew in Christ Jesus, so I can do the good things He planned for me long ago.

— Ephesians 2:10 nlt

Reflection...

_____

_____

_____

_____

_____

Flight of Fancy

Now, you're going to study this photo of a passion flower and look at how beautifully it is formed, how intricate and yet how bold and majestic. I want you to picture God sitting by an open window in a little cottage surrounded by His floral creations, and standing right beside the passion flower vine is you. And just as God studies and smiles when He admires His passion flower, His eyes move to your face and He studies how He made you and He smiles with pride. *Another beautiful creation*, He thinks to Himself. "I'm especially drawn to that one," He whispers to His passion flower, "and I can't stop admiring My handiwork." Remember, you are of greatest value to the King of the Universe. When you think about yourself or look in the mirror next time, see the passion flower and remember how He is constantly thinking of you and how proud He is of you! Repeat out loud: "I am His beautiful one, made bold and majestic, and filled with God's creativity in my heart and mind." Now, close your eyes and step close to the window of the cottage so God can admire you!

SCRIPTURE

"But now, O Lord, You are our Father; We are the clay, and You our potter; And all we are the work of Your hand."

ISAIAH 64:8 (NKJV)

PRAYER

How can I thank You, Papa God, for the beauty of Your creativity? You have called into existence all that surrounds me and painted my world in unbelievable colors and given me an amazing variety of landscapes on which to feast my eyes. And then there is me, a human being created by Your hands through my parents. How masterful are my intricacies and I am fashioned after You! Thank you, Lord, that You desire to look on me as a wonderful example of Your handiwork!

Losing Stress

I know we've had a reading regarding de-stressing your moments, but in our world, it's so easy for stress to find its way back into our daily routine — I think we need another *stress less* imagination transformation. We visited a beautiful forest the first few days of reading, but it's purpose was finding a *new you.* Today, we're going to revisit our forest and leave our stress behind.

Imagine yourself walking in a wooded, wild place. There are towering redwood and giant sequoias all around you as you crunch on the leafy carpet…releasing the smells of moist earth and decaying leaves. You feel like you're in a quiet, ethereal place where you can feel God's presence. Take a deep breath and feel God's peace wrap around you like the morning mist encircling the treetops. (Do this now, close your eyes for a moment, breathe deeply and "see" yourself in the picture I've just painted for you.) Now, I want you to smell the sweetness of the air. Take five slow, deep breaths and give your tension to Jesus. Picture yourself putting your tension in a small silk bag with a drawstring at the top. Then find a low hanging branch in your imagination and hook the ties over the branch. Then walk away.

Papa God, Jesus, and the Holy Spirit are like the towering trees in this special picture. They are full of strength, always surrounding you and accepting your stress and tension anytime you choose to give it to Them.

Thank Them for their constant presence and return from the wooded, wild place refreshed and ready for your day, or ready to close your eyes in peaceful sleep.

The Lord is my shepherd; I shall not want.
He makes me to lie down in green pastures;
He leads me beside still waters. He restores my soul.

— PSALM 23: 1-3 NKJV

Reflection...

_____
_____
_____
_____
_____

Flight of Fancy

Close your eyes and, for five minutes, imagine yourself in this wooded, wild place and see yourself doing the actions I described in today's reading. Now, paint your woods however it pleases you and don't forget to take along your special bag to put your stress and tension into when you are ready to hang it on God's limb. Enjoy yourself and let your imagination go!

SCRIPTURE

"The Lord gives His people strength; the Lord blesses His people with peace."

PSALM 29:11 (HCSB)

PRAYER

Thank You, Jesus, for being my strong tower like these towering trees. Thank You for Your patience as You are always willing to wait for me to realize I can give my burdens and stress to You. Help me learn to walk under Your canopy of love, provision, protection, and peace.

Chocolate Delight

Today, we're going to imagine my favorite food in the world...cho-co-lot. You notice I've misspelled it in order to emphasize how much I love it...a *lot!* We're going to heaven today and visit God's kitchen as He prepares a special dessert time just for us and it's calorie free...heavenly! He loves to do things that bless His kids. Remember, you're coming with me as my special guest! Start your "imagine-engine," here we go!

I see it, there is the big sign on the Pearly Gates, "WELCOME TO THE GREAT CHOCOLATE FEAST." Below that, it says in smaller letters, "WELCOME EVERYONE, INCLUDING THE CHOCOHOLICS TO THE ONLY MILDLY ENTICED NIBBLERS." Can you smell it...? Like a candy shop...like Mom's special hot fudge sauce...like brownies baking in the oven. Oh yum! Better do a chin check for drool!

Welcome to the Great Chocolate Feast!

"Look!" I squeal. "Will you look at that kitchen? It's ginormous! Marble and gold counters...shining silver stove, oven and utensils that sparkle in the...hey, there are no lights on...oh, duh...we have Son-light." Nothing artificial here! I'm giggling now as God and Jesus both have aprons on and chef hats and big smiles! Can you "see" that? They point us to the buffet table to begin our feast! The table is so long I can't see the end.

Oh my, it's unbelievable and right in the middle are two of the most gorgeous chocolate fountains I've ever seen. One is smooth milk chocolate and the other a perfect dark chocolate. There is every kind of cookie, cake, brownie, roll, candy, and drink imaginable set out for our enjoyment. Plus, next to the chocolate fountains are a myriad of choices of things to dip into the flowing chocolate. There are enormous strawberries, raspberries, blackberries to dip that are about three inches long! There are pieces of banana, pineapple, marshmallows, big coconut flakes, pieces of buttery pound cake to dip, and much more. My mouth is watering...is yours?

I look around and see I'm first in line and *you* are behind *me!* I'll try to leave you a little! I need a plate! A vision of beauty that's hard to describe and to actually see shimmers close to me, and suddenly, there is a crystal plate in my hands and a pure gold fork. I smile a "thank you" in the direction of the shimmer and catch a glimpse of a sweet smile in return. Shaken but not deterred, I move forward and begin to gather my chocolate treasures. It's the most amazing thing...I turn to you and say, "Does your plate keep expanding? No matter how much I put on it, there is always a little more room and yet the size of the plate stays the same and all my goodies are there!" You nod in the affirmative and we both smile. Yep, it is definitely heaven!

Finally, we're ready to sit down and eat. We're led to a little table for two, just you and me. There are two gold goblets of icy cold milk...for what goes better with chocolate? We utter a prayer of thanks and begin the best dessert feast of our lives. We eat slowly, savoring each bite with a sigh. We can't believe we've eaten it all and, strangely, we don't feel stuffed or sick of the sweetness. It's God's miracle gift to us, we realize. No calories, no weight gain...only God giving us a gift just because He wants to make us happy today.

That's our God, always wanting to bless us more than we can ask or imagine! Now, today, or tomorrow (depending on the time of day you are reading this), I want you to seek out someone and bless their socks off... like God blesses you!

Reflection...

_____

_____

_____

_____

_____

Flight of Fancy

As you read above, you've taken an imaginary walk around God's banquet table of chocolate. I want you to close your eyes now and recreate the scene above in your mind. Be there. Walk around and look, smell, and taste to your heart's content. Then look over in the corner and see God's face as He watches you enjoy something He made just for fun and pleasure…just for *you* and *me* because He loves *us!*

SCRIPTURE

"Now to Him who is able to do exceedingly abundantly above all that we ask or think [imagine], according to the power that works in us, to Him be glory in the church by Christ Jesus to all generations, forever and ever. Amen."

EPHESIANS 3:20 (NKJV)

PRAYER

Thank You, Jesus, for giving us special times of joy just because You love us, Your kids, so much!

Feeling Forgotten?

*B*efore we go one step further, we need to clear up the devil's lie that you are forgotten, unseen, and unimportant. *Wrong!* If you have accepted Jesus in your heart, you are His child, you are seen, you are important, and He knows your name! Now *that* is sometimes hard to imagine…the Creator God of the universe knows your name, my name!

Today's reading may be a little hard for some of you as we're going to spend some time in front of our mirrors… either actually or in our mind. Either way works because you know what you look like on the outside even if you're not looking in the mirror. But we're going to "imagine" the *new you* based on what God sees on the inside. And we're going to make some declarations, out loud, to our mirrors!

The Creator God of the universe knows your name!

First, believe me when I say that God looks at you, His child, and sees only the beauty of His creation. Now yes, of course, it's true that we can "let ourselves go," but that is surface stuff, we can handle that later! I want you to concentrate on what God sees inside…what you have the potential to become…but all the while know that He loves you for who you are now, at this moment, with an unfailing love.

Now, get ready to declare *out loud* into the actual mirror or the mirror in your mind.

Say,

"Thank You, Papa God, that You have made me brave."

"Thank You, Jesus, that I am healthy in mind and body and becoming more so each day."

"Thank You, Lord, that I am an overcomer."

"Thank You that I am in the right place at the right time."

"Thank You for making me a creative thinking and doing person."

"Thank You for providing all of my needs."

"Thank You, God, for filling me with unreasonably optimistic hope and faith."

"Thank You for allowing me to be a light and encourager to others."

"Thank You for giving me wisdom to discern lies from the enemy so I don't accept them."

"Thank You, Papa God, for Your unfailing love for me, even me, just as I am."

You can see why God loves you so unabashedly, so passionately…listen to all that you are, can be, and will be! Now give yourself a big smile, because you are fabulous! And remember, He knows your name!

Reflection...

_____

_____

_____

_____

_____

Flight of Fancy

You're on a roll now. Declaring builds up your faith and hope muscles. Repeat these declarations again...*out loud!* Perhaps you can think of other things to declare out loud. Make declarations a way of life and watch your faith, hope, and joy grow.

SCRIPTURE

"Now we see things imperfectly, like puzzling reflections in a mirror, but then we will see everything with perfect clarity. All that I know now is partial and incomplete, but then I will know everything completely, just as God now knows me completely."

1 CORINTHIANS 13:12 (NLT)

PRAYER

Thank You, Lord, for knowing my name so that I can declare out loud that I am not forgotten! Lord, I purpose to make declarations a part of my daily routine so that my faith will increase.

Flying Free

Did you ever have a dream that seemed so real you could feel it happening? I have a memory that was stirred to life again because of a dream I had some months ago. I dreamed I was able to fly, like Superman, but the flying was contained to my high-ceilinged living room. In it, I was able to just step up into the air and be lifted up. Then I would hold out my arms and begin to swoop down and up and across…swoop down to the floor, touch it with my foot, and propel myself back up to the ceiling. It was magical and I was giggling and laughing and having so much fun. I was like an anti-gravity ballerina and it was heavenly! There was a euphoric feeling of freedom, release, and daring as I tried new tricks of flying. I remember trying to talk to someone to join me, but I couldn't see them. Then I woke up and remembered it all with clarity and thought to myself, *I really did that once!* Then I told myself I must be crazy, but I could remember the feelings I had while flying!

We cannot limit the God of the universe to our tiny sphere of experience

So, I began to pray and ask the Lord if I was crazy or was this an actual memory of something real. Jesus brought to my mind the time in 1992 when I almost died from complications from surgery. The evening of the surgery, after I'd recovered from anesthesia, my husband said he visited with me for a time and I seemed to be fine. He said the nurse came and gave me a shot of morphine for pain and to help me rest through the night. Seeing that I was drifting off, he left for the evening. To this day, I have no memory of that time frame.

The next morning, he found me in ICU on a ventilator and unresponsive. Apparently, a nurse's aide who had come to draw blood early in the morning found me not breathing! My roommate told my husband that everyone began a furious activity. I was strapped to a backboard and whisked away. Obviously, the medical team got me breathing with the help of the ventilator, but I was not doing well. My husband said, when he arrived, all the nurses and doctors backed out of the room like they were giving him a chance to be with his dying wife. Prayer chains were set in motion and he began to pray and call out loud for me to come back. My first vague memory as I reentered life was of a voice calling me from a distance, "Cheryl, come back, I need you, the kids need you." Over and over, I heard that voice calling me back. Finally, the voice became louder and I opened my eyes, saw my husband, and tried to speak. But there was a tube down my throat, so I couldn't. There were joyous tears shed and praises to God going up. Within a few hours, I was back in a normal room and went home a day later and made a quick recovery! My condition was attributed to a very bad reaction to the morphine.

People have asked if I had an "out-of-body" experience and I used to say I couldn't remember one. But I believe that God showed me in that dream that my "flying free" was the "out-of-body" experience for me. For I remembered flying for quite a while, then suddenly, I stopped as the Lord allowed me to hear that voice and make my choice to respond to the calling.

We believe that I am a miracle. It was a strange event and other's details of the story showed that I had not been breathing for some time when found by the aide! But now I have no fear of what lies on the other side. I've never really been afraid but more curious of what happens when you die, or almost! I believe that the moment we step even temporarily into "the other side," we experience total peace, joy, and even fun if we've given our heart to Jesus and are one of His kids. He loves us so much! I'm guessing that the story I've shared might really have pushed your imagination to the limit. But we cannot limit the God of the universe to our tiny sphere of experience or parameters.

Flight of Fancy

Now, ever since that reminder dream, I've often gone back in my imagination to my flying time and what a hoot! How fun to imagine having the ability to swoop and soar and tumble through the air, just playing. As adults, we don't play enough! So, I want you to play for a few minutes before you go off to sleep or get ready for work. And know that God, Jesus, and the Holy Spirit are on the sidelines watching your antics and laughing with joy as you relax and "play"! Oh yes, and imagine yourself in a nifty flying outfit. In my dream, I was wearing a striped green and white shirt and stretch pants...not much to look at but that's what I had. I "imagine" you can do better! Now smile and *fly!*

SCRIPTURE

"The streets of the city will be filled with boys and girls playing in them."

ZECHARIAH 8:5 (HCSB)

PRAYER

Thank You, Father, that You want me to experience the joy and freedom You gave us to enjoy.

Singing Over You

oday, I want you to imagine what the voice of God, Jesus, and the Holy Spirit sounds like. I'm sure we will all have something a little different. For me, when I think of God speaking, I hear a deep, resonant voice, but laced with kindness. The kind of voice that makes you get crinkle lines by your eyes from smiling. For Jesus, I hear a smooth, baritone voice with overtones of gentleness. And for the Holy Spirit, I hear an almost breathy whisper, like water running down a gentle slope of stones in a brook. How cool would it be for the three of them to sing a song of love over you! Can you imagine the sound of the perfect blending of tones and the background of the Holy Spirit?

Maybe you're thinking, *The Lord is way above and beyond singing over me...I'm hardly worthy!* But remember, the God of the universe shaped you in your mother's womb and you are special to Him. **You** are the **one!**

So, now you're probably wondering what words could They possibly sing over me and you can't imagine any. So, I'm going to help your imagination. Here is a little verse I want you to imagine the Trinity singing over you...you can hear any melody you want, just see if you can picture and hear Them singing this:

You are My child that I wake to see each morning,
And for you I bring the sun up at the dawning.
Live in My love today, I'll be with you all the way.
I'm always here, I'm never gone, In My shadow you belong.
And this, child of My heart, to you is My love song.

Remember, the God of the universe
shaped you in your mother's womb
and you are special to Him.

Reflection...

_____

_____

_____

_____

_____

Flight of Fancy

Read through my instructions here, then follow them! See yourself sitting or lying under the canopy of a weeping willow tree, because at the end of your "flight," this tree will be weeping at the beauty of the magical moment you'll be "seeing." Your eyes are closed as you rest and relax there. Now you begin to hear beautiful harmonic humming and your eyes pop open. There, in front of you, are God, Jesus, and the Holy Spirit...you recognize them instantly (no matter how you picture them). They are smiling at you as They begin to quietly sing this song over you. Your eyes fill with tears of joy, peace, and contentment as you see the love in Their eyes for you. Now close your eyes for real and put yourself in this picture. If you can't remember the words I wrote...no worries, They will have even more beautiful ones for you. Now, as you finish your imagination session, can you feel the misty tears of the willow as it weeps for the glory of the enchanted moment it shared with you? Live loved!

SCRIPTURE

"The Lord your God in your midst, The Mighty One, will save; He will rejoice over you with gladness, He will quiet you with His love, He will rejoice over you with singing."

ZEPHANIAH 3:17 (NKJV)

PRAYER

Oh, dear Papa God, Jesus, and Holy Spirit...how I thank You for loving me enough to sing a song of love to me and over me! You have filled my heart with peace and assurance of Your great, everlasting love for me. Thank You that You have made me worthy!

The Color of Joy

What do you imagine when you think of the words *"joy"* or *"joyful"*? A place? A state of mind? An emotion? Do you also connect it with other words like "happiness" or "contentment"? Have you ever thought of what color you would paint joy? Do you realize that joy is connected to your health?

Today, I want us to paint a picture in our minds of what joy looks like and what color or colors you link to it. For me, I see the color yellow with silver sparkles sprinkled on it. Yellow, to me, is such a cheerful and freeing color. As children, we're always taught as we begin to get old enough to color a picture that the sun is always yellow! Right? I think that's

Have you ever thought of what color you would paint joy?

because the gasses, energy, and light emitted from the sun are so powerful and "shiny." Those elements may fall into the color spectrum of what we identify as yellow. Good choice!

I know there are moments, days, weeks, or even months when our joy is overwhelmed by stressful situations. Some of these situations are of our own making and some have come to us unwarranted from our enemy whose sole purpose is to "kill, steal, and destroy" (John 10:10). It takes a choice, sometimes a hard choice, to trust Jesus and give Him control.

I think that joy is a choice, whereas happiness is more of an emotion. I believe that, even in times of sadness or unhappiness, we can still choose to live in an overall state of joy. I also link joy to contentment. In the Bible, the apostle Paul said he had learned to be content in whatever situation he found himself in…and he was often in very unpleasant situations! Now, is this easy? I think not in general. But as we learn to rest in the love of Jesus, there we will find our joy. We must continually visualize Jesus with a long pole across His shoulders and buckets hanging from each end…that's where you must lay your burdens of the day or the moment. Let Him carry them and you find rest in trusting Him to carry them! Then look around for joy!

Studies have shown that laughter is actually beneficial to our health and God fashioned us in such a way that our bodies respond positively to joy and laughter. In Proverbs 17:22, it says, "A joyful heart is good medicine, but a broken spirit dries up the bones" (HCSB).

Reflection...

_____

_____

_____

_____

_____

Flight of Fancy

Read then do. Close your eyes and imagine the color you want to paint joy with. Then imagine scenes, people, situations, objects that bring smiles to your face and your heart. You can even make up a little story about what you see as you splash them with your *joy color!* Now give thanks to Jesus for allowing you to see all the things in your life that bring you joy! Live in healthful joy...by choice!

SCRIPTURE

"But let all those rejoice who put their trust in You; Let them ever shout for joy, because You defend them; Let those also who love Your name be joyful in You."

PSALM 5:11 (NKJV)

PRAYER

I choose joy, Lord! Help me to remember each day that it's my choice how I view my day and my circumstances. Fill me up, Father, with overflowing joy as my faith increases belief in all that You have for me.

DAY 30

Holy Spirit

Today, we're going to really put our imagination to the test as we try to imagine what the Holy Spirit would look like if we could see Its or His or Her presence physically. The Word says we are made in Their image... male and female He created us (Genesis 1:27). So, maybe the Holy Spirit has female characteristics! Since we know God is the great *Imaginator*, I believe He can have the Holy Spirit represented in a myriad of shapes and forms; in the Bible, the Spirit was sent as a dove and another time as tongues of fire. Can we really limit how God chooses to show Himself...through Jesus and the Holy Spirit? I stand on the scriptural truth of the Trinity, Godhead of three in one. But though the three are one, they are also individual. So, in keeping with the tenor of this book of looking at things "outside the box," in this encounter, I may refer to the Holy Spirit as "Them, He, She, It, or They/Their." If this makes you uncomfortable, just change the wording according to your choice, but don't throw out the baby with the bathwater. Allow yourself to participate in the joy of using your imagination to "see" the Holy Spirit in your own way during this encounter!

You are His treasure so let your picture of Him be your treasure!

In my imagination, I often think of the Holy Spirit appearing as something like shimmering gold and raindrops mixed together. There is a body-like form but you can see through Her. There is brightness shooting off the edges of Her form and She floats instead of walks. I imagine the Holy Spirit as somewhat elusive...but always around you even when you can't see Her. I picture the Holy Spirit as constantly hovering, vibrating, and creating new avenues for us to explore in our hearts and minds.

I can also imagine the Holy Spirit like a rippling brook, constantly in motion but also reflecting light in all directions. But this moving stream of water is not only around me, I can picture It living in me like the Scripture says. This living water brings instant calm to my being when I tune in to listen to what the Spirit wants to share with me.

The Word says the power of the Lord dwells in us through the Holy Spirit (Acts 1:8). And in every imagined picture, I see the face of the Holy Spirit as serene yet strong and unafraid, wholly confident and sure of His actions and position as part of the Godhead. I see a smile dancing at the edges of His lips, like He knows a secret about me — something He likes!

As you can tell, my imagination can "see" various pictures of the Holy Spirit! Whatever the Holy Spirit looks like, the main thing to remember is that you are infused with God's Spirit if you have accepted Jesus as your Lord and committed your life to Him.

Reflection...

_____

_____

_____

_____

_____

Flight of Fancy

Now, it's your turn. Close your eyes and let your imagination "see" the Holy Spirit. Feel the Spirit's presence as His eternal love encircles and surrounds you. Imagine His joy as you accept His love for you! I encourage you to write down how you picture the Holy Spirit in your journal or on a slip of paper to keep in your Bible. You are His treasure, so let your picture of Him be your treasure! Of this you can be sure, the Godhead — all three in one — loves you beyond measure, however you picture Them.

SCRIPTURE

"Repent, and let every one of you be baptized in the name of Jesus Christ for the remission of sins; and you shall receive the gift of the Holy Spirit."

ACTS 2:38 (NKJV)

PRAYER

Thank You, Holy Spirit, that You can be to me exactly as I imagine You...a beautiful image that comes to my mind whenever I think or pray or talk with you. Thank You, Father God, that You allow me the freedom to picture the Holy Spirit in terms that I can wrap my head around. Thank You for living in me!

Creative Vibrations

T his is the last reading in our imagination devotional, and today, I'm going to share something with you that may stretch your thinking cap! My husband and I recently became aware of a book and video called *God Vibrations*[1] by pastor/teacher, Dan McCollam. Absolutely amazing! (I'll reference it for you later). The bottom line is, science shows that everything in the created world vibrates, even inanimate objects. In a teaching DVD about vibrations, Pastor McCollam played the sound of the vibrations of Jupiter and Saturn and the star system Alpha Centauri and the sounds were captivating. Each is totally different! And the fantastic thing is this goes

Always remember, when God speaks Life happens!

along with how God created the world! It's way over my ability to explain this in detail. But in listening to the DVD, we learned that while scientists have known that each person's DNA has a particular, unique makeup like no other person, it's now known that each person's DNA vibrates distinctively. Scientists and music gurus working with sound were able to put music to a string of DNA and produce a "song" that we can hear. On the DVD, we heard the song produced for the DNA of a swan, then several others. He said that each DNA's song will last from eight to fourteen minutes, depending on its vibrations!

I began to weep at the beauty of the swan's song I was hearing and was overwhelmed with the reality that God really did sing over us when He

[1] **Dan McCollan, *God Vibrations Study Guide: A Kingdom Perspective on the Power of Sound,* (2013).**
Also in available in DVD series and workbook.

fashioned us. Can you just imagine what the sounds of creation must be like? There are scriptures throughout the Bible about nature groaning, trees singing…

All of this new (to me) truth sounds like something absolutely imaginary. Then Pastor McCollam took us back to Genesis 1 and read about how God spoke the world into being. Spoken words vibrate the air even though we can't see it; there is so much here to ponder and think about. We must remember that each word *we* speak also carries power to give love and build up or to destroy.

But for this moment, I want you to know that, when you speak to God, He hears you distinctly as He remembers the music of your voice and the way He created you as "one of a kind." I can easily imagine God singing over you at the moment He began your creation. *You* are *very* special! Always remember — when God speaks, life happens!

Reflection…

_____

_____

_____

_____

_____

Flight of Fancy

Now, I want you to imagine what your DNA might sound like! And picture God singing over you as He created you...starting with giving you a perfect heart, then designing your unique face and features. The whole time, the vibrations of God's fingers are fashioning you. Imagine God's smile as He was making you and hearing the sound of *you*. Your sound is unique and God recognizes your sound. Isn't that amazing? Now sleep in peace or enter into your day knowing that, wherever you go, you are bringing the sounds of Heaven's music to those around you!

SCRIPTURE

Genesis 1 – Read the entire chapter and see how often it says, "God said..." (NKJV)

For example

In verse 3, *"God said, 'Let there be light...'"* verse 6, *"God said, 'Let there be a firmament...'"* verse 9 *"God said, 'Let the waters under the heavens be gathered...'"* and on and on.

Commentary

It was the power of God's spoken words that called everything into being. And since we don't know exactly how each thing was finished, I can imagine that, as God called things into being, they may have needed a little "tweaking" to get it just like how He wanted. For instance, after God created Light in verse 3, the Bible says in verse 4 that God saw that the Light was good but then He **divided** *(made a few changes to make it better)* the Light from the darkness. God had a plan to make the whole of creation perfect! As God saw what He had created, He realized it "was good." Remember that He created **you** with the same precision and *you are good!*

PRAYER

Thank you, God, that You made us to ever seek more of You and to learn more about the majesty and miracle of Your creative genius. Thank You that I can ponder and think of how powerful were Your spoken words, as the very act of speaking set vibrations into motion which created the world. I'm reminded again how the Bible speaks of You breathing into us the breath of life...the act of breathing setting into motion other actions which brought life! So much, Lord, there is so much we don't know about You. Thank you for giving us minds, hearts, and imaginations that can guide us into a closer relationship with You!

After Words

*W*ow, I'm thinking that, by now, you may qualify as a certifiable Imaginator…at least I hope so! After coming along on this journey of learning to think outside the box, I pray you have learned to use your imagination to rethink how you view God and your world around you. Along the way, I hope you were able to laugh during some of your *encounters* and maybe shed a tear or two along the way. My goal was to state thoughts and concepts in words and ways that were unique and perhaps made you want to reread a sentence, just so you could really imagine the word pictures I was painting on the page. I hope there were times when you said, "Oh, I loved how she stated that thought because I could picture what she was saying."

I also hope that this won't be just a "one-and-done" reading, but that there were messages on certain days that really resonated with you, or that you loved participating in a few Flights of Fancy so much, you want to do it again. I also hope you will recommend this book to your friends and family or give this book as a thoughtful gift.

But mainly, my prayer is that you have grown comfortable using your imagination. I believe God wants us to dream dreams of goodness, joy, love, and laughter. He wants you to walk with Him as the powerful person He made you to be.

May this be the beginning of a new way to live…being unafraid to imagine and dream. However, remember also some of the lessons about the power of the spoken word and commit to speaking life-giving words to yourself and everyone you meet. Reiterating what I wrote at the end of Day 1's reading, I pray that you've now entered a new level of communication with God and that your taste for life will never be the same.

Special Note: Perhaps you've never asked Jesus into your heart to be your Lord and Savior. It's so simple to become one of His children. Wherever you are, you can simply pray (I suggest out loud) and tell Jesus that you repent from the sins of your life and that you believe He is the Son of God. Ask Him to come and live in your heart and take control. Tell Him you're ready to turn around and begin a new path with Him. Welcome! Jesus and the angels are shouting with joy over your decision!

May God bless and keep each one of you in His tender care!

Cheryl

CPSIA information can be obtained
at www.ICGtesting.com
Printed in the USA
LVHW080954011118
595277LV00005B/1/P